Red Truck Bear

Red Truck Bear

Poems by

Richard Nester

Cover design by Venetta Manson

ISBN: 978-1-950462-74-2

Kelsay Books Inc.

kelsaybooks.com

502 S 1040 E, A119
American Fork, Utah 84003

Acknowledgments

My sincere thanks to the editors and staff of the following publications for first acknowledging the poems (and previous versions of the poems) in this manuscript:

Addiction: Swallowed the Moon and Doused the Sun: "Hooked."

The Catholic Agitator: "Who"

Floyd County Moonshine: "Chestnut Culture."

Poets Facing the Wall: "My Exit."

Praxis: "At the Gym," "Clean."

Rise Up Review: "Cherokee Nation," "Empathy," "Leverage."

Shelia-Na-Gig: "Tally."

South Florida Poetry Journal: "Closure," "Eden."

Contents

1

Space

I've never met a moon
that wasn't in plain sight.
Astronomers say
that the new one circling Neptune—
Hippopotamus or something—
is one of those plain sight moons,
like ours.
We look at it
and it looks back with no
discovery on its mind at all
and even less concealment.

Academy Suite

Academe 1

Language is trouble—
a thing I've learned from ape shows
on PBS, and humanity is less
a category
than a direction,
east or west. We never
meant to imitate the world;
we just caught ourselves
doing it, miming
the slow words living
gave us until they stuck—
not garden, but grove,
groove.

Academe 2

We couldn't leave well enough alone:
first the grove and then the cloister
and later the apple of patents—
ivory towers like silos of learning
with just enough grass to grow
something, provided we didn't kill it
first by holding it too close. How
many elephants would have to die
to raise an edifice of tusks? How
many rhinos, how many gorillas,
murdered for their soft hands
because the world wanted ashtrays,
their hands like monk-hands,
cramping in the cold of iteration.

Academe 3

How like a family the human family is,
especially so in how we treat our oddballs,
exceptionals, refuseniks who can't play well
with others but show us who we are
by standing apart. If they would only invent
something, we might leave them to their work.
But what to do when they turn dangerous
and start inventing us? Give them a garage
and go away or lock them in the attic—
we can't decide—and give them hell
until we give them awards.

Indecipherable

I'm impressed by poets who can make a big deal
of the smallest moment. It encourages the rest of us,
the non-poets, that what we're doing matters. In fact,
it makes reading poetry into a kind of prayer.
If God isn't listening, then at least some poet,
somewhere, is, or has listened, at some time.
Given that sort of attention, nothing is quite as worthless
as it appears. Of course, they have to convince us.
Just telling us it's so won't do. For example, today
I'm shredding my father-in-law's medical records.
He's been dead six years, his ashes buried in a cemetery
two miles away, but my wife is convinced that his
dead identity might be worth stealing in a way
that could implicate us. I'm not convinced,
but my wife is a poet and so has powers far beyond
those of mortal women, especially when she's insistent.
The papers go in a slot and come out like noodles
from a pasta machine, accept that now they're indecipherable.
My father-in-law was indecipherable, an absurd combination of
angry wit and genuine witless despair that you'd never want
to stand close to or investigate anymore than you'd stick
your hand into this shredder, which, unlike my father-in-law
stops when it overheats. A real poet could make
something out of this that would convince you of your own
indecipherable worth, beyond the misunderstandings,
the disregard, the tedium, so you can go on and not give up,
the way you keep threatening to, for whatever reason.

Reception

In those days, TV had to convince us
it was real—*One Life to Live, Days of Our Lives,*
You Bet Your Life, This is Your Life—
stories you could hitch dreams to.
Instead of *go west*, it was *stay put*.
If the set broke, it could be fixed like
a wagon wheel or a car or someone who was sick.
It would be picked up and gone for a few days
as to the hospital, and you'd be lonesome
until it came back, forced into going outdoors
to make a life out of sticks and chores—
narratives that had to be cooked, like dinner.
I remember the poses we got into
trying to turn ourselves into antennae,
trying to separate an episode's plot
from the TV's liquid snow.
But it was impossible to be a part
of the reception and watch
at the same time—medium and message.
I'm older now and I know more people
who can't come back no matter how much
I have to tell them or them me.
It's a hard mix, the right amount of real.
Which is why TV was compelling,
all plugged-in and still exquisitely lonely.

Storm Quiet

Whenever I see calligraphy, I thank God
I wasn't born in a place where Chinese
is spoken. I would never have learned to read.
Wherever I see it, on placemats or greeting cards,
in art museums, or on chalkboards—
about to be erased—my head swims.
So much poverty and plenty all at once.
The word *writing* is not enough.
"Picture writing" we call it.
But what stops a *roof* from being a *bird?*
A straw here or there in a cacophony
of straws, the skill to distinguish *villages*
from *villagers*, *stars* from *skies?*
Impossible! I need a language where letters
become sounds become words become sentences
and not this sudden leap into. . . *thingness,*
like a storm, the too sharp reality of the page,
its sudden fury and stillness. In war, disguise—
in madness, landscape.

Film School

Tony Perkins in the movie *Psycho*
observes that the expression "eats like a bird"
is a misnomer. An unremarkable, remarkable remark,
though less noticeable than the creepy music.
Try driving on a rainy night to that tune.
And yet his observation is the perfect placeholder
for a tale of bottomless desire
and how things aren't always how they appear.
It lures us back inside the frame,
toting our suitcase sense of the normal.
In truth everything in the movie is normal,
a virtual hardware store of normal, except
for its seemingly random, outlandish announcements
when too few of something is suddenly upset
by too many. How like our own impatience
with routine and how we make a totem of grief,
our desire for society and the cleansing
wonder of conversation. If only God
would make a walk through now and then
and stop teasing us with the undependable
shadows of birds or the infrequent kindness
of humans. Then we might more easily accommodate
the simple horror of living.

Nougat

A teacher once told me that all writing
is rewriting and that all reading is rereading.
If that's true then maybe all watching is re-watching,
and the movie that most perfectly expresses
this truth is Hitchcock's *Vertigo*. We watch it again
and again and again and still can't tear ourselves away,
unable to grab its sticky, radioactive essence
until it grabs us—the distinction between hunger
and need, surface and substance. The plot's
sweetness loves him, Scotty, only in so far
as nougat in a barrel, bag, or box that we pay for
on the way to our seats, on the way past and to
our temptation—the Mary Jane, Jujube. Sugar Babies
that will rip the fillings right out of our teeth—
loves us. Our truth staring plainly from the screen.
We will do anything for a taste.

Developmental Psych

Teenagers think a lot about death,
and who can blame them
when dying a virgin is still a possibility,
a constant threat and cause
enough to be especially distractible
or at least fussy over dinner?

If not already at the center,
adolescents at least hope there is one,
a counterweight against growing
evidence of breakage.

Imagine my outrage
when I learned, years later,
that my youthful idealism
was merely a stage,
a common feature
of a developing frontal lobe
and not unique.
My rarest hopes reduced
to something hormonal—
an issue of tissue—so to speak,
hot flashes, a property
of the race, not scars
but text.

Ponder or Pander

Once, I wrote a one-act play so awful
the fact of it still sticks in my craw.
Having meant to draw a snake, I drew
instead a hat. What's up with that?
And yet was pleased upon production,
having others enact my treasures, my inmost wishes
served like dishes. Was this what Shakespeare found—
dressing gown as dress—pulling his dozen vectors,
or was it more akin to the pleasures
of porn directors?

Dream Sex

My Friend Tells Me Her Dream

In my friend's sex dream, the
mannequins wear fur coats and the orchard
is heavy with apples.

"Where is the sex in my sex dream?"
she asks. *Ah, there it is!* The two of us like apples
in a bowl the size of a bathtub

drunk on the available laughter,
my love, with his affordable hips, and me
without my rain coat.

I Tell Her Mine

In my sex dream
Donna X finally kisses Freddy M.
I direct—moving the extras, the lights, the cameras.
I tell them to wait, but they don't wait.
I tell them to stop but they don't stop.
The cast cheers and claps.
In my sex dream there are longings
that daylight can't erase. They stick to me
in pieces, the way confetti, soaked
by celebration, sticks to the streets
after a parade. . . It's funny how hard it is,
nearly impossible, to dream this dream
or any dream, all the way to the end.

Wild

Forsythia arises from a mating of kudzu
with barbed wire. The only thing that can make it
worse is to give it thorns. Add the mobility
of tumbleweed and it becomes a demon plant,
a zombie, able to swallow whole towns. Forget
its pastoral sham, its yellow spring explosions.
What starts as green twigs, bird-nest stuff, ends
as thick branches, fat as a skinny woman's wrists,
and mean as a bad marriage, a paradise
of bird-shit that slashes cheeks and whips
eyeballs from sockets. Your yard becomes
a prison yard—beware of shanks. Forsythia
hates you, the way Republicans hate wildlife.
You've heard their slogan—nine words, three
commands: *burn it down, kill it off, use it up.*
Hornets are forsythia's hired thugs.
You think you've got troubles. Stick one
forsythia sprig in fresh ground and wait.
I've seen forsythia devour houses and spit out
the bricks. It will eat your dog.

Underground

Winter—life in the hayfield
and in the yard. I can tell from the hummocks—
a civilization of moles—their mole equivalent
of the late Egyptian, their tragic
and their comic Nile.

In summer their tunnels bow
the ground, not enough to pitch the mower
over, but enough so I begin to imagine
I'm in a rodeo and curse them.
I know nothing

of mole life and do not wish
them well. I only know they're tough and smart,
especially for midnight beings
at home in the dark. Still, I don't
suppose they're good for grass—

their upside-down harvest.
And yet? Why suppose a mole's life
is shapeless poverty. What about their care
for young or their rabbit-like urges?

Human stories are full of the subterranean—
rivers, glades—a fascination with our own
dark ends, the way we tunnel through
our dreams, births and deaths in hand
like luggage. It's not unusual for us
to start a meditation in sunlight and come out
god knows where, our silly mole-song
of ships, starlight, and stars.

Phobia

Since fear is a fascination,
I'll say she fascinates me, the spider
in the window box outside the kitchen window.
How she does it in the cold I'm not sure.
Something about being dry I suspect.
I don't plan to look closely. If she
was indoors, she wouldn't be
indoors long. Not if I could help it.
Outdoors, I'd say we have a truce
but that implies the impossible—understanding.
Her understanding is that she needs to hide
as much as she can. Last summer
I got a taste of how that works.
I saw what looked like old webs outside
the glass, knocked them down and washed
the windows, which were dirty anyway.
Next morning the webs were back,
rewoven perfectly with a certain patina of age
so they looked abandoned.
How does one make a web like hers look
abandoned—ramshackle? Only a gut
genius could do it. Overnight, moths went
for the kitchen nightlight like cars
for a filling station and this mother spider
would snag them, nibbling wings and feet
and feeding her nearby young.
If it weren't for this gut fear of mine,
I might have been in awe.
She'd even leave an old moth or two,
paralyzed by venom, half-eaten, hanging
in the sunshine like a prisoner
caught in stalag wire.

When the kitchen light was off,
she'd go back to work and rebuild her webs,
and in the daylight disappear.
Biology is all the truce we have—
feeding and re-weaving. It's okay.
I have friends myself—
birds too build intricate beds, and they eat
spiders—whole.

Forsythia Again

One year the hedge fought back. It was harboring
      hornets, the way an aircraft carrier
harbors jets, and I was stung fourteen times in as few
      (or as many) seconds, depending
on how you look at it. I counted them later in the bumpy
      mists of a Benadryl fog, each one
a parable of rage. Now the yard work only keeps the house
from appearing deserted. Though I don't know why this matters.
      Dad says that we get too many visitors
anyway, but I'm here, one thing on my mind. If the forsythia
      isn't cut back soon, I'll not see
         our red pick-up again.
It will rust behind the garage door like a ruby below ground,
      overgrown with vines drunk
         on photosynthetic zeal,
its fuel tank pregnant with solar heat, buried, compressed,
      and buried again like a grudge.
Nothing spells dispute like territory, and this one is going
      nowhere, save toward greater weariness.
Nothing tears the soul like trying to find a way back
      that will let you come forward
along a different path, yourself but better. It's a fool's
      equation—what equals what.
The world is more full of justice than we know.
      But it hurts.
    What's fuel now has been fuel before.

Crossing

Brokers in TV commercials—
Smith Barney or E.F. Hutton—try to convince you
that investing is rational, and it is, as far as it goes.
Betting the ponies is rational too, as far as it goes.
You get your racing form, and you see who runs well
in mud and whose workout times are rounding into form,
and you hope no one else sees what you see
so the price stays low compared with the pay off.
The track takes a cut, which you don't begrudge,
since without the track, there's no race.
It's not the track you're betting against.
It's the other bettors, which is odd when the crowd
stands and cheers, as if it had one voice
when it doesn't. Rooting for luck, I suppose.
Everybody roots for luck. But you don't
because you've studied the form and know there's
no such thing. You're rational, and know too
that there are good bets that don't win—the price of
crossing judgment with circumstance. Truly
telling a sure bet in proof's absence, is impossible,
but that's the bottom line of rationality—its price—
devotion and devotion's cost.

My Dementia Stricken Mother Asks Me to Wash the Windows

It didn't make any sense
to wash windows the first week in March
when the air was so cold
that it summoned a banished sort of emptiness
through which forgotten segments of winter
entered, more benign than a burglary
but as unwelcome. Not that
we endured any special suffering
just everyone in the household wondering
why now. It's not my favorite thing,
making a stir, but impulse is impulse, to be
respected because it's—*impulsive.*
But you have to be careful.
Too much cleaning up
and one starts to see dirt everywhere.
I left some specks
in one of the high corners
for proof.

Clean

Clean is the world's invitation to dirt
as if you've put out a shingle—open for business.
Mess this up.
My mom was the other way around—
dirt invited cleanliness—
with the pressure and persistence it took
to make *clean* happen.
She could make already clean objects sparkle
as if bringing out some embedded principle
that made the things she touched—happy.
They would shine like gospel in a new revelation
of personal *thingness*.
It was like that when she came to California
from Virginia for visits.
I didn't want her to have to cross the country
to clean, but I was helpless.
For weeks before, I'd scrub everywhere,
but there was no beating her.
In the first minutes it would happen,
her starting up, and not with any reproach either,
but with a sort of industrious
joy—her way of feeling connected.
I had tried at least, and there was no reason
to feel bad. At least I was standing next
to devotion, even if I wasn't there yet.
Which is maybe what dawn thinks each day
as the light comes up—everything
can be restored. Restored.

Red Truck Bear

It never fails: however big a story you've got,
somebody else has a bigger one. I was putting
gas in the pickup when a man at the next pump,
waved me over. He wanted to show me something:
two dents—both small—that a bear
had put in his truck by bumping it with his head.
Just like this, he said, hitting his forehead
with his hand. I wanted to warn you, he said
since you've got a red truck. Bears hate red.
I supposed that was bulls, but he said
that when it came to butting, it made
no difference. He was still telling his story
when we went inside to pay. The woman
at the counter said a bear had nearly rolled her car,
putting $2400 on her insurance. What kind?
I asked. Just a bear, she said. No, the car?
A grey sedan. God bless the red-truck bear!
He must be a teller of stories, I thought,
the way he worried himself bumping
his head into something he couldn't budge
but still knew enough to stop and what
he shouldn't bother about at all.

2

Small Town

Lewis Burrell
was a chemist so talented
that he could lay out drunk for three days
and not get fired.
Rocket secrets were in his gas tank
in his pocket on key rings
by trinkets in his mother's jewelry box
in the dust on his mantel
in his brain
and all the folks at the Arsenal could do
was call his home
and beg
his wife to get him back to work.
It's a tale my father tells,
who rode to work with Lewis twenty years,
amazed
that such foolishness could happen.
He does not guess
that I am in his story, floating ghost-like,
that Lewis read Lowell and Yeats and Dylan Thomas,
that I am beside him watching
the Miss America pageant on a spring night
and hear him say
I am the saddest man alive
before he passes out.
Poems cannot assuage the truth
nor would my father believe it had he heard,
nor I, in my young pride as guest,
have guessed.

Tally

The cost of what's lost is never clear,
some say one thing, some another.
Nearness matters, for good or ill,
and how one counts,
or can count, or is willing to.
I tell my wife I count on her. It's true
and I was happy leaving the single life.
Once and gone was all there was to that.
Still is (and glad). The best goodbyes
are thought of as simple exchanges,
the unparsed, uncalculated *next*
with its hopeful blue blossoms.
But nothing happens without cost.
New ease when it's new can be unsettling,
its stiffness unfolding. If that's all there is,
be grateful. The long, uncertain burial
of some things progresses forever, or is progress.
An image sticks in my mind: my mother
shuffling flowers in a vase, the one *hand*-thing
(of many) she still likes to do, does almost
compulsively—clipping, pruning, now satisfied,
now not—making a mess on the kitchen floor.
Very uncharacteristic of her, that willingness
to make a mess. Dementia's gift to art.
My father lurching out the door on his cane.
"I've always hated that man," she says to me
(a little stunned but not surprised)
then adds, "who is he?"

Grudge

Grudge

No one survives this place, not really.
Eventually our own hatred topples us, brings
us back to earth. But that's okay, it's worth it—
this house, this company, our commitment.
We pass like strangers, which of course we are,
nothing coming of nothing, whether
in the two big chairs or in the hall.
It's the best outcome, nothing: two sets
of loyalties, sheltering in the same place,
two ribbed, angular hearts below a roof
of ripped beginnings, each one at the same sill
gazing outward, bemused by yeasts of separation,
fake stares, unspeakable commerce.
I wanted my father's love, he wanted my respect.
Neither of us got what we wanted.

Caves

There was a caddy at my father's club
named Jack, a kid just out of middle school.
My father called him "rainbow" because
he'd learned that Jack's granddad had carried
a flamethrower at the battle of Iwo Jima.
It's not the sort of thing that you forget,
the slow advance of tiny men, Marines,
up the side of a seemingly vertical mountain,
foreshortened by distance, streaks of flame
that looked like rainbows to my dad, each one
a promise of return, the promises adding toward
the summit—columns of hope that ran from cave
to cave, each one of them worth a cheer, if
he'd had the time.

But there was work to do
among his shipmates, unloading barrels of explosives
down a slick ramp. The ship had run in close
enough to shore to take Jap mortar fire,
each miss pushing plumes, a splattering of sand.
That much he told me but no more than that.

I've accused my dad of being
dead to wonder, as if he had a phobia for anything
that might amaze or startle. My friend, who knows
Greek, even made up a word, *phavmaphobia,*
which translates as "fear of the new or strange."
It's not the sort of question one asks—
what memories of home were in an enemy's mind
or on his walls before they turned to ovens.
He recalls my son's birthday, August 14,
by reference to the day of Japanese surrender,
forty-five years earlier. Going home
was rainbow enough for one life.

Bad Charity

The most begrudged charity that ever was,
was my Dad's. He'd roust me out of bed for it
on weekends, missions pulling neighbors
out of snow banks, then listening to him grouse
the whole way home about what losers
they were for getting stuck in the first place.
I wonder what he thinks of me
behind my back. A lot he'd claim, I suppose,
if you pushed him. But then I make my living off
the government, teaching English to foreigners,
not the sort of job he could respect, not like
plumbing or pumping gas, or handyman work.

With those jobs he could get something for free
without having to give anything in return.
Once he threw my brother's friend
out of the house for being "cheap."
"King of the freebies" he called him.

We were White Americans and so immune
to the chummie nicknames he liked to call people
that he'd met in the service, names he was sure
they would like—like Dago somebody or Wop or Pollack,
nicknames he was sure they wouldn't mind
because people in those days knew
they weren't racist.

He still enjoys calling a Jap, a Jap,
since it helps to level things for Pearl Harbor,
the same as Manzanar or Hiroshima, with no need
for apologies. If you think a thing is right
at the time, he claims, there is never
a need to apologize. You can't apologize
for history or to the dead.

He came to think a lot of my aunt Hazel
in later years because she'd helped him out
with Mom's dementia, but Hazel was a loser
for the longest time because she'd married a drunk,
the first time around, and a wealthy man
for his money on the second try.

Two suspect marriages.

From time to time I think of myself
as part of humanity. How foolish. I should know
better. You can't be a part of anything
that large. I'm a part of my family.
That's all—my father's son—
because that's all there is
to be part of.

Stepping Back and Breathing Deep

My father only wanted two things from me,
ever. Either I would be a successful golf pro
or I would have been killed in Vietnam.
In the first case, he could follow my live career
and brag about me to his golf buddies
and know that he'd been responsible.
In the second, he could look at my picture—
my never-aging photo with the clean-cut,
self-saluting cap—and piss and moan
about the country that had deserted me
and know for sure that it hadn't been his fault.
I'm sorry. I never should have said this in a poem,
much less read the poem in public. I've embarrassed
us both. But otherwise this stuff keeps circulating
like a lawn chair in a cyclone, more likely to kill you
than make you comfortable.

Griot

What do *griots* think about when they remember?
I would say that my father is a kind of griot,
without the fire and smoke of ritual remembering,
but I don't know what *griots* think about.
Is it just a person's facts, without their flesh,
what can be housed in a mailbox. Or is it more?
In *Roots* there were bits of legend, Kunta Kinte
going out to make a drum and only returning
after three hundred years of slavery. My father
wouldn't remember things like that—plot twists,
complexities of character, failings of spirit.
Those sorts of things might cross his face
like shadows, and I don't see them.
No shade. If anyone in his memory were to starve,
it would be from an iron certainty not hunger.
Perhaps his anxiety about really knowing
anyone is that he might forget what he considers
their important facts, losing them
as one would a tree in fog or something slimy
by a creek bank. Better to remember what was cruel,
than what was fun, or if not cruel, indifferent.

The More Things Change

Like a crow scavenging a ham-salad sandwich made by the church
ladies of my mother's
church for her memorial (great lady that she was), a memorial
being the modern substitute
adopted by geographically spread families for a funeral, wherein
rites of visitation and

internment are divided into parts that play out over time, his
scavenging witnessed later from the
kitchen by my brother and myself, who could not eat the overflow,
but fed it to the birds,
while our cheapskate father, as usual, played cards of sympathy
and social class to get others
with far less money and position to continually to do things for him
as they have always seemed
to, behaves much like a crow, squawking from the far room, wary
and fretful, wanting more.

Foreign Policy

Yesterday, my father asked me if mainland China
was still called Red China, and I think he was dismayed
when I told him that it was just China now. After all,
the Chinese are still foreigners and if their foreignness
can be distilled into the single adjective, *red,* so much
the better. It's true that we buy a lot of their products,
but no cars. Who would buy a Chinese car? If only
our manifest differences could be expressed as two
completely separate globes, one for them and one for us,
then we could leave the bad insects and the toxic sunsets
to them and be safe like we used to be. He asked me
after sitting down to read the newspaper, which he has done
cover to cover for a long time. He's asked me this before,
ever since the grandson of a war buddy—
now deceased—went to China on a church mission.
He married a Chinese girl, and now that they have a child,
the three of them are coming to America. "It's just China,
Dad," I tell him. The truth had never been so easy.

Leverage

The day finally came
when we were ready to do it,
move the whole earth
just as Archimedes said we could.
We had the lever
and the fulcrum too,
our great will wedged
against the purchase
of our heart's leverage,
which is what one tries to get
in any trading of this
for that.
And still we held our breaths
because of what we feared—
a tumble—
what one gets sometimes
when fractures stack like plates,
one on another and another,
in series, because we knew
at bottom the one law
that can't be got around—
broke things stay broken—
even sacred objects
and have to be cleaned
one breathing bird
at a time.

Empathy

If you put a spoon in a bowl of sugar
and move it slowly enough around and around,
you'll get an image like the one I've seen
on the TV news lately, or maybe
squirting Reddi-wip in a hot cup of cocoa
works better. I don't know.
I'm not Mister Wizard. But I begin to wonder
how small I'd have to be
for the sugar's surge to whirl me dizzy
or how large before I'd be able to ride out a typhoon
and not notice its passing, the way
flies ride out whispers.
Whatever size I was would be my home
as sure as an Eskimo's igloo
of ice and snow or a Laplander's hut—
my truth, my universe, like my hat size,
even though I don't wear hats.
I read a brilliant essay once by Stephen Gould
about why the fifty-foot woman in the movies
couldn't be shapely.
It was. . . sobering, erotic in its own way,
but clearly down to earth.
They say the devil is in the details,
but the devil may as well be God—
ruler of both ends—
for all the good imagination does.
No wonder justice, with its itty-bitty seed
of empathy, is so hard.

Conned

Who

He's George Corey Wallace, race-baiter,
in the sheep's clothing of jobs and national renewal,
standing in the school house door
of a segregated school. Before he's done
there may not even be a door. After all
what good is education if it only makes for
a less fearful electorate, more wary consumers.
We've learned that fear can be bought
and sold like any commodity, sand to stick
your head into and smother. Who is he?
The man who shot buffalo from the back of a railroad car,
plunderer of the female land from his high perch,
scion of the rich, deceiver of the poor, a warrior
who never left his arm chair, criminal
sharpie. You know his name already,
like you know the apple of our national DNA,
our too human birthright, the flame of our fear
that can only be doused from where it starts
by an act of will. Start now.
Start yesterday.

Counting

The Rockettes don't want to dance
for Trump's inaugural but they have to.
It's in their contract. What little girl
whose biggest wish was to dance
would have expected this? It's not
the sort of thing one plans for
any more than leaving one's home
because bombs are falling.

They've bombed Aleppo for months—
one two three—and bombed too
underground
under the Great *Indivisible* Plains
to squeeze out the last drops of the dinosaurs.
When you see Trump on TV
watching the dancers, try to see
if he's counting—one two three kick—
and so on, and ask yourself whether
America is getting its money's worth
in long-legged women
in fighter jets
in all the purchased bytes and bits
that have little in common except
that they can be counted and compelled.
Let the sound of counting ring
in the land with its dead motions—
one, two, three—
so many hurts, so many deportations,
every asylum displaced
in the binary glare of inspection.
I don't count.
If he wants this poem, he can have it—
for nothing.

Vigilance

I've heard it said that advertisements are
the new poetry, the truthful hyperbole
of the sales pitch and the brochure.
West Virginia,
they took your coal
and left you the black lung,

and what they did to you, they're doing now
to every bleeding state and inner city,
the old now-you-see-it
now-you-don't shell game
of subtraction by extraction,
your wallet, your soul.
Ads work *en masse* to steal.
Poems work in the single heart
to restore—original ore.

Secret

The dirty little secret of history
is that it's safe or appears so,
a blanket of rubble
to hide under
as humanity goes fetal
in a private, merciful apocalypse,
a shout to the hovering
helicopter of the future,
arms raised,
I'm here—
take me, take mine,
I was.

Mandalay

I recall a statement Malcolm X made
following the Kennedy assassination, one he later
regretted, about chickens coming home to roost.

What form his regret took I don't know.
Whether he saw what he'd said as impolitic—
as Elijah Mohammed suggested—or whether
he had embraced a larger sense of national
and human sorrow? But I understand his original
anger and cynicism. America (a geographic region
he was born into but not in any way his country)
doing injury to itself—a sort of karmic justice—
the kind Lincoln talked about when he opposed
blood drawn with the lash to blood drawn
with the sword in his Second Inaugural.
                              Jump cut—
the Texas School Book Depository morphs
into Mandalay Bay, another mentally disturbed,
lone gunman barricaded in a room, except
no Italian 52mm, Carcano model, infantry rifle now—
three shots in 27 nearly impossible seconds—but
rather an NRA approved/provided—like a pimp
provides a woman—assault rifle with a legal
bump stock attachment, ten inescapable minutes
to work with, a clear field of fire and ten thousand
rounds of ammunition, spewed from fortress height,
shooting up, gunning down a crowd of, no doubt,
many NRA-endorsing, confederate flag wrapped,
country music fans. America doing injury to itself.

Is it really an aberration when it happens so often?
We've been shooting each other for a long time,
and always with cause, some half-baked, maniac reason—
close up or at distance—accounts beyond settling.
I know what you're thinking. Now is not the time.
A hundred years ago perhaps? Two hundred? More?
The unexamined griefs of slavery coming home to roost.

America I hate your thoughtless vindication
of yourself, my country, me, your constitutional free speech,
free thought, hand-grenade going off inside my head,
my heart. You see I like country music too,
which must mean that I've been shooting and getting
shot myself—in the belly, in the chest—for years
every time I laugh in faux sympathy with Haggard's
"Okie from Muskogee" or play along with "Trouble in Mind,"
aping George's fiddle with my harp.
                                    It's one country,
so don't tell me you're not implicated, mad enough
to shoot back or be shot by every gunman since Oswald.
I'm as much a child of hate as you are, defenseless
every time I write about what seems impossible—
that justice could take this long.
                                    So angry that I refuse
to care anymore because I already regret everything.

Hooked

Everything that lives is addicted to something,
if only sunlight—the seed dressed in time like a yolk,
outside will, the seedling's asphalt-busting arrow.

We're all at the starving end of something,
begging for one more sip—love or danger,
a just-so neatness or the hoarder's fortress of trash.
Art is a waste of time without obsession, and picturing
humanity minus its addictions is impossible.
But none of that is what we mean by hooked,
the choice that chooses you, the tag
that means you're it, forever.

Thirty years ago I quit smoking,
and for twenty years I had dreams so vivid
I'd wake and not believe I'd really quit. So I know
that quitting can be done, but I also know that sometimes
it can't. Jenny Diski, my favorite writer of memoirs,
dead of lung cancer, which is why I've never felt heroic—
just lucky, and the most important reason I never
light up now. I might never get that lucky again.

Hooked, hooked up, horny for tomorrow.
Buddha's take it or leave it disinterest
ain't my style, a jokester, in the court
of whatever's next. Dylan's skinny declaration
of love, echoing in my ears, " I never asked much/
I never asked for your crutch/ now don't ask for mine."
If you need it, heed it. But be the chooser,
not the chosen.

I had my reasons for quitting collected
for a full year before I stopped. They were too
much like my reasons for smoking—theories.
The worst thing you can have in life is a theory,
a tape that runs over and over till you stop
noticing the new and different. That's another thing
addiction is—a theory, an explanation, a bill of goods
you bought when your resistance was low—
not the key but the lock. Justifying ain't quitting.

Frederick Douglass said about himself
in the narrative of his life in the passage that
begins "there stood slavery. . ." freedom
far away and slavery familiar, however terrible:
the best description of bondage I've read
though he wasn't talking about chemicals;
telling us why it was so hard to bust loose
and why even after years of freedom
he "felt [himself] a slave."

The leap is always physical even when
it's spiritual, a two-fisted patience. He had
to beat his overseer half to death, and you
will too—the master in your skin.

There's one more thing I want you to know—
how much I loved it, the family rituals and the
comradeship of fellow smokers. Loved it as
drinkers will, not drunks (abased, degraded),
but drinkers in love with liquor's great romance.
I can't number the problems cigarettes solved—

packs a day of problems. Even now, when I see
cigarettes being smoked in movies, I feel a sense
of communion. To leave that was loss—
the hardest thing—to be exiled, self-banished.
Homer's sirens were but a book-story compared
with that. It was woven in my nerves.
Tell me what you want to be free of,
and I will tell you all I know about how to do it,
which is next to nothing: bite hard on the hook
of something you love that loves you back
and doesn't lie.

Nation

Look Ma We're Pocahontas

My wife insists I have Indian blood,
citing details of my appearance, her way
of trading my milk-pure German heritage
for something more glamorous,
which is what I sincerely thought,
until this book shows up in my family library,
Life in Rock Castle, Virginia: in Their Own Words
by Michael Ryan, a park ranger, with its chapter
about the peoples of Rock Castle Creek—
Native American and European—who shared
the intimate richness of game and fast falling water
and the chestnut culture—my ancestors. If the genes
weren't mixed late, they were mixed early.
Anything else wouldn't have been human,
the human making of stories beyond the reach
of history's slice and dice. My question is how people
could send kinsmen on a thousand mile journey
of exile without batting an eye. Human?
And whose words? Damn few from Indians,
that's sure, although their faces and pieces
of faces show up in photographs that can be studied,
mined, the way my wife studies my face of an evening
or studied the face of my grandfather years ago,
whose brow, she says, looked like it came off a nickel.
DNA, starving and sticking, is the hungriest
substance there is, and names are not just groups
of syllables. Did the grandmother of Pocahontas
call her that or was her appellation mangled
in the invader's mouth or on his pages? That's my
other question, along with this one. What do we call
a tree that forgets the buried, fuzzy millimeters
it climbs from? Firewood.

Cherokee Nation

They were almost us, our dark equivalent—
too close for comfort—and we were almost them.
They planted crops, invented writing, read Scripture.
We thought their women beautiful.

Asia had come east across Alaska;
Europe, west across the Atlantic. They met in Tennessee,
the missionary from New England and the shaman from Red Clay,
and almost recognized themselves. *Almost.*

Worse than our diseases, our political intrigues,
was the invention of history, its constant displacement.
We taught them property and stole it.

"The meanest work I ever did was moving
those damn Indians," an army private wrote from his outpost,
on the void between *almost* and *never.*

One hundred eighty years to the east,
at a desk in Virginia, reading John Ehle's *Trail of Tears,*
I wonder what to keep—not this desk surely—
nor these tears, which are too late.

What none can carry.

Chestnut Culture

Once money grew on trees—
not tens and twenties but nickels.
What my calculus teacher said of functions
was true of chestnuts, the woods are—were—
full of them, littering the forest floor
each fall. Found money.

There was a country store
at each end of a six-mile gorge—a tall hike—
but whichever way you went by the time you got there,
you could buy a pair of shoes.

Culture is what arrives once habit spills over,
a sky that fills with clouds until the clouds rain and restart.
Culture is what you hardly notice but can't do without—
hindrance or help—what you think is forever—
a bounty unprayed for, umbilical or chain.

How we cried when they left, whole forests wiped out.

To say that we took them for granted is to say too little.
What buffalo were to the plains Sioux, chestnuts were to the hills.
Without them, the work went underground or indoors.

They were human, these trees,
with a human extravagance, and yet like gods or caretakers,
their leaves whispering wisdom, cooling thought.
Philosopher trees. To live under them
was to live. . . *Deeply.*

They were good for everything
but firewood—too much air in their seams.
One man said he wanted a coffin of chestnut
so he could pop and crackle his way through hell
like a one-man *oompa*.

Still standing, they were too big to burn
and too old to care. They were too *too*.
No lover has ever loved us like the chestnut did.
Now we are on our own and lonely
like we never knew we were.

Science Method

According to John Ehle, the Cherokee never felt lonely
because they never felt alone. But how does he know?
Was he there? The medicine men told him, I'm guessing.
Their stories, the ones we translated, told him. How could they
be alone with the squirrels chattering and the water
and wind in conversation and the deer in dialogue?
Yes, this was Eden after the naming, we thought.
This was the Garden! This was how
we converted the shaman's words. But how would
the shaman have known before the white man showed him
what it was that we aspired to, envied, hated: the unfathomable,
the indescribable space between the self and the world?
Curious, the shaman might have asked what this *thing* was
we touched, brushing our hand across a void he couldn't see:
our answer, our gift, only the gray form of a penetrating ignorance
we were proud of. Better to have a steel knife blade,
the shaman thought, with an edge neither stone nor water,
one that would not leap up and cut one's own heart.

My Exit

for Amiri Baraka

The word *existential* has been kicked around
so much lately that it hardly exists. I learned it
in high school, reading off the syllabus—
Sartre and Camus, *No Exit* and *The Plague*—
when the word meant something, at least to me.
An idea made real by acts is what it meant *to me,*
and not our usual prefab guideposts of doctrine,
tradition or genetics. I'd had enough of those,
stained-glass sermons with their clapboard
precepts, and in my DNA , the boarded-shut
postures of relations over family dinners,
my family, who weren't immigrants any longer.
We'd been here too long, long enough to forget
when we first learned English and began to move
among our fellow citizens as though we were natives.

I learned about this reality teaching ESL
to California kids from Asia and Peru and Slovakia,
who stamped my passport. America has always existed
better in the minds of its immigrants than anywhere else,
in the blue suits of the Irish Iron Brigade at Gettysburg
and in the black and tan bodies of Negroes at The Crater
in Petersburg on their way to liberating Richmond.

Donald Trump has re-branded *Amerika.*
Have you tried to read his signature? If you didn't
know who it was doing the signing, you'd never
figure it out. It's a wall. At least, John Hancock—
the insurance guy—who owned hundreds of slaves,
peacock though he was, wrote a hand
that could be read.

In nightmares I dream that I'm a Democrat
congressman forced to vote for THE WALL
in order to get DACA. Then I realize I'm awake.
Blake told us, an idea can be a wall too,
once you've erased its human components.

Existential was a part of something I could call myself,
though not in public (just me speaking to myself like
an understanding friend), trusting its too cool but ever
faithful feel—more real somehow than being a Methodist.

Now it seems forever joined to the word—*threat.*
I'll leave the South for the last time when my father
dies—his "existential" death, my exit.

3

Westward

Like everyone else in America
we came to California, young and green,
because we were tired of apocalypse.
How ironic is that? My wife and myself
in a beat-up Datsun, busted radiator,
Tom Joading it across, in flight from families,
a family to ourselves, without birth or flag.
We broke down in Arkansas and got help
by the roadside—riverside—years ahead
of the cell phone. How was that possible,
a future in our trunk, every moment an epic
episode? We must have believed. Nothing
but belief could have done it. Several Americas
later we're still here, getting a happy
phone call from our son, who has passed
his CSET (whatever that is) on his way
to a teaching certificate—amazingly fearless,
hateless—in what seems an age of both. Empires
are hard to live in or leave—ask the classics—
Rome, never consumed, always on fire.

Feeding

You'd have to see it to believe it—
a photo my wife showed me off the internet—
a big-eyed bug, probably a mantis,
staring at the camera through a hole
it has just eaten in a leaf. Humans have spent
a lot of copy trying to describe what distinguishes us
from other creatures. Mostly we've been wrong,
the smartest among us as wrong as the dumbest.
Even Shakespeare, who according to Bloom
"invented the human" was only parroting a line
he heard about our proximity to angels.
As far as its content goes, I'd say that the photo
captures a quintessential moment of evolution—
consumption, which is bigger than sex even,
since you've got to eat to live and live to fuck.
A baby bird's first thought isn't about sex.
The hole that the mantis has eaten has created
a frame around its face—a white background
like a matte for itself in an otherwise green surface—
as if it has taken a selfie. Is self-regard the human
hallmark? Perhaps, but then it might be fairly common.
Lawrence describes frozen birds falling "stone-dead"
without a trace of self-pity, which makes them superior,
praiseworthy. He didn't know. He thought himself
praiseworthy too to have seen it and described it well,
which is maybe a sort of bird-like preening on his part.
Everything preens, self-grooms. I've heard the view
that the universe has evolved humans just so it can take
a kind of selfie—the self-important stars shining down,
on us, centered here, munching our green hopes.

Survival

The autumn burn pile is smaller than usual.
It's a matter of notice, less concern for appearances
equals less trimming, more down-creep than upkeep.
The flames are almost cute, like movie-set flames.
Another cataclysm no one cares about. Some minutes
after the match, a semi-roasted beetle bumbles out, black
against the green grass, trailing his little Hindenburg.
All matters of death are matters of survival as well.
Even death knows that. It's tacked to his wall
like a slogan, rules for metabolism and burning.
Reaching for a hose, I spot the beetle, dry grass
catching around him, as much from memory of heat
as heat itself, yet needing to be assuaged, lest grief
and rage at such an end consume us all.

Eden

Suppose the animals got to sign contracts,
not just for themselves but for their species,
for all time—the original Daddy Rabbit
bunnied up to the table with the Lord Most High,
First Car Salesman or whatever name he called himself—
what would the deal sound like? First, it's written
in a language we can't read. But I'll translate.

You're prey, see, and there are predators,
which sounds nasty, but there'll be sex all the time,
and you can eat as much as you want. No kidding.
Have you ever seen a fat zebra? I didn't
think so. Okay sign here. Keep the pen.

What got me thinking about this
was an idea Jefferson had that there ought to be
a new Constitution, a new contract, every twenty years—
the length of a generation. He liked fairness and this
seemed fair. No one in bondage to the past.

Madison showed him how it really is—
even in science—no true cohorts, measurable just
by themselves, unto themselves. Rather
everything overlapping, everyone
on everyone else's toes.

We sign what's put in front of us
for good or ill and do the best we can
without the gift of a fresh start.

My day and yours and the ever-stupid sun.

Protein

I understand why humans are such thieves—
the bunch of them. It's in their DNA and their diet.
Humans are stupid, but their DNA is smart.
It looks at cows grazing all day, and chickens pecking,
and says to itself, I couldn't live like that.
I'd rather be lost in thought under a tree, by a river.
Instead of eating what they eat, I'll eat them.
I'll steal what they earn for myself, as if I was
in business—the theft business. The Sufis knew it—
poets are thieves and every human is infested
with poetry. You may as well trust me as trust
yourself. You and me, with our perpetually dark insides
craving light. Never tell a story with your back turned.

Call Me Cassini

The Cassini spacecraft is due to crash September 18th.
That's what my wife says looking up from her iPad.
What's it crashing into, I ask, not having stayed current.
We can see it at the Beckman auditorium in Pasadena, she adds.
But where's it crashing? Surely not in Pasadena.

No answer. By then she's onto something else,
a tidbit about the San Diego Zoo, which is why I accuse
her from time to time of being "scatterbrained," something
she admits. It's in both our families, a kind of gravity
we're aware of, that holds us back, if not down.

In any case, I'm not driving north for two hours
on crowded freeways when I don't know where it's crashing.
You can journey a long time through space
without hitting anything, but when you crash,
it's always into something, which usually doesn't suffer

as much as you do. Which reminds me of my early
romances. Women—girls really—breaking up with me,
alleging I was in love with love and not with them.
It seemed a mere excuse to me like the cliché
it's not you, it's me that people use when
they don't want to tell you the truth.

You can't crash without crashing
into something—gravity's consequential, stupid end.
Each time, I was a long time getting well—reprogramming.
But I never argued. I just put their rebuke in my pocket
and walked away—still standing.

The Last Straw

The whole courtroom would understand
but the law wouldn't, and I get that.
You can't divorce someone for leaving
those skinny plastic things
all over the house, the kind they use
to tie the tags on store-bought clothes.
It's not a public offense, the sort the law cares about,
but I care. It's amazing how often I look down
only to spot one, nearly invisible against
the rug, trying to trip me—visually,
psychologically. She doesn't do it
to drive me crazy, but, hey, crazy
doesn't care. She gets great bargains,
I'll give her that, and she's thoughtful too,
enough to hand me a scarf when it's cold outside
to warm my lips and chin. But mostly
I think it's to shut me up.

Another Life

for Kay

Will loved the fights. Each Friday night he'd sit
white-knuckled in his favorite chair, watching
the gray screen jab and flutter into life.

"Look sharp, ta-da-da-da-da.
Feel sharp, ta-da-da-da-da."
I'd drag my dolls around the floor
and watch him watch.

Lula never liked the fights.
At least that's what she said.
Fingering her rosary, she'd wait
soft-faced until the brawling drew her out,
then form a kind of mob all by herself,
yelling for the underdog and blood.

She favored Bishop Sheen,
his Sunday lectures on the trinity—
super-ego, ego, id.

The fight cards junk and jumble now
like broken toys in a box:
Kid Chocolate fought it out with Sugar Ray
and Two-Ton Tony battled with the Rock.

With all his teeth and minus half his thumb,
Will survived to ninety. I loved the way
his mangled, workman's hands would brush my cheek.
Lula's heart, a punch-drunk fighter, finally blew.
Death won on points.

We walk the ancient neighborhoods, my child and I.
"Who's your favorite boxer, son," I ask,
spotting a set inside above a bar.
"Magic Johnson," he says. Whose face
is this that greets me from the window's glass?
Whose memories are these that bob and weave
but do not blur? I love them still.
Loss keeps no calendar.

Narcissus

The magazine
with my poem arrived yesterday.
It was beautiful. I opened it to my page
and left it open all night,
and when I woke, I stared at it for a long time
before breakfast.
I didn't shave but I didn't want to.
My poem was the only mirror I wanted.
I wasn't there in any way
a stranger would notice, but I knew
how to find myself.
The *me* on this side of the mirror is mere
facsimile. Outside, the leaves grow lonelier,
invested in their windswept quarrels.
They have been like that since I fell in.
My virtues and sins have swapped places,
my poem like a menu in the café of myself.
So what if the picture promises more
than what is on the plate?

Lap Time

They knew I was one of them,
the snot-nosed kids at my son's day care.
It was supposed to be our time, his and mine,
before I went to work, my last chance
to read him a story. But we never got the moment
to ourselves. As soon as I'd sit down, they'd come,
a pack of zombies, creeping and climbing,
backing in with their infant plagues,
their sinister infections.
Like most zombies, all they wanted
was love from the sound of my voice and the warm
words they got from a book in my lap.
It was disgusting.
All we wanted, my son and I,
was time
to ourselves away from the world's troubles,
and here they were
right in our laps, with their punk versions
of the big picture, as plain as if they'd come direct
from television, snot-nosed kids
with their need for notice—
which is all love is when it starts.
Notice me. . . *me*. Eventually, my son
got tired of sharing what we had
and told me to just go on.
No more reading. I guess he knew
the world would get us soon enough.
It always does.

Not as Hopeless as It Seems

Before reading *Anna Karenina,* you'll need
to decide for yourself, whether you really like novels.
If you don't, don't start. It's about adultery. At least
that's what I decided a few pages in. An easy guess
Just like every country song, even the ones about family
circles and homes on high. They're all taking positions,
for it or against it or what to do in the midst of it.
Even the ones that don't mention adultery. That's how
it is when you read a good novel. The world becomes
that thing—all of it—even when it's not—the way
in dreams when we lose our keys and cars and minds,
only to be glad to wake up and find they're still there,
along with the night stand. I don't mind frigates
taking me "lands away." I just wish they'd pay more
attention to bringing me back. But one has to do that
for one's self. Later on, I read a novel almost twice as long,
War and Peace. Perhaps I'll write a novel myself
and call it *The Big and The Little.* If I could do
that and keep you interested, I'd be Tolstoy. Its shortest
sentence is two words, "drops dripped." But it takes 800
pages to get there, and without the right translation you'll
miss it, the signal loneliness of the drops. You must know
what the listeners in its pages know. A battle is coming,
a breathless one, with death's beauty and horror, its surprise
and patience. I've crossed America four times by train, each time
by coach and traced the coast of California twice, sleeping hard,
on this elbow and that hip, wishing my knees belonged to
other legs. I couldn't have done it without a book.
Without a book it would have been impossible to picture.

Moments

I Knew

This morning I looked at a tree
and was glad
it wasn't a star. Had it been
a star it would have burned me crisp,
instantly. Faster even.
I felt that much kinship with it,
the tree. It too was glad,
and I knew
it was happy about the light.
I'm a tree, it said,
and can move
large stones, slowly.

Woods Walk

Today I felt very animal.
I can catch something, I said,
with my large hands
and quick eyes.
The rabbits ran away fast,
but I don't think they were scared.
He's writing a poem, they said.
We're safe—
as we always are
after the wolves have eaten.

Moon

The big moon, bright and full,
is so
big that my eyes
get bigger just looking at it.
It lives in a place so
cold that degrees don't matter.
Is it so
bright because it is so cold?
Or the other way around?
One look is all it takes
for me to freeze.

Reckoning

I can't name them, not one,
but they're always there, around daylight,
stirring their stew of voices.

Suburban birds, at home
around humans, their eaves, their garages.
It must be a good place to have drawn so many
to that corner, awash in song,
like a Charles Ives concert—a bird ballpark
or stock exchange.

I play my harmonica at the bus stop
on my way to work and wonder if they care.
None of our tunes cross or coincide,
although occasionally they stop singing all at once.
Probably the cat, not me.

My work days aren't unfriendly,
just long. From dark to dark some days
with a soul ache in them—
akin to sore feet.

Small hurts that are hard to rub out.
Not enough to stop me but enough
to make their own tune—
sore foot sonata in E minor.

What do they teach me, those birds?
To reckon myself as they do perhaps—
of little consequence beside important song,
as by a great river.

Appearances

We cut pokeweed from around the threatened barn,
a jungle of them, taller than a man. It wasn't a job
that needed doing, the barn no longer
a working barn on a farm not really a farm.
But it made a better picture once they were cut,
enough so the neighbors would think us industrious
and not give us up, not this autumn at least.
We pulled the cut stalks into the shed to dry
so they would weigh less when we finally
hauled them off to a corner of a distant field.
Meanwhile, the green berries continued to ripen,
unaware they were no longer part of a living plant,
their rampant purple staining our hands and clothes
as we worked. Rabbits ran from the pile where
we dumped the brush, and I wondered whether
the poke berries made good eating for rabbits
or if they would leave them for the birds.
A hint of frost lives in every green thing—
if you live by the juice, you die by the juice.
Fields fertile and full of injury. Granddad's
homemade wine, its purple a poke-berry purple,
its fox grapes sweetest in dry years, because
the vines are in a frightful hurry to be elsewhere.

Wine Country Prayers

No thermometer convinces like cold weather.
What cold believes, you believe.
What it accepts, you accept.

Frosts half a year, fog piled to the sky's edge,
until it looks like snow, Orion prowling the sky's black
alleys like a cosmic cop. The land

takes its beating and delivers its testimony.
Its bible is commotion, vines living with or without soil,
with or without faith. From the grape's

point of view, the world is a winery,
every year a dry year, and we are birds. Grapes swallow
life's vacuums and spit them out like seeds,

looking for cracks. Their greatest worry
is how to move, their roots looking down the way
our eyes look up, the way

a child's eyes penetrate goodness
as if it was common. Pray for them, for all those,
at whatever border, who must surrender
their sweetness to live.

A.I.

As if the present, semi-real world
isn't dangerous enough, we have to worry
about household appliances revolting.
It could happen.
Your slow cooker strikes a deal
with your just-purchased domestic security system
and together they, access your credit.
Before you get home, they've made
the dog an offer it can't refuse, the vacuum
has snorted your meds and the door
is locked.
Double agents are one thing—
the occasional Mati Hari flashing by—
but crossing species takes a make-do you don't have.
Diplomacy is not your strong suit.
If being human isn't knowing best and feeling
smug, what is it? Out the window
the sun shines like a falcon spitting dimes
for a cosmic jukebox, the car
radio murmurs something about the Seychelles,
and a different song climbs the charts.
But don't mind them, the machines,
their innocent criminality. Give them time.
Soon they will be human.

Closure

I saw on PBS how the circle closed,
finally, neatly from its first beginnings
in the Eocene—horse and man.
The two of them were hiding
in the dense growth waiting for the world
to dry, the big-eyed one who could climb trees
and the ground-dwelling one with four toes.
The dinosaurs had all burned up
and the world was suddenly minus masters,
open to climbers and scamperers.

Then it began, earth crafting their romance—
man and horse—like a poem, without knowing,
without intention, merely the line's desire to taste
itself, to raise its head and look.

What a fine thing I am, the line thinks,
bending this way and that, as if it has a brain.
Maybe it was only how the cells hooked up
but it had power—life's sexual gravity.

Two social animals walk into a bar
and walk out with each other
into time's bordello, alley, bedchamber.

Horses can't breathe during strides
like we can. They risk so much running full out,
like whales diving, surfacing high from being
breathlessly below a long time. Each horse
stride a deep dive into the future.

We were in love so long without knowing—
man and horse. We needed their speed and power.
They wanted our hands.

At the Gym

for Kristen

Another early morning lifting weights.
I lifted one two three thousand pounds
and lifted them again—
a ton and a half. I lifted myself.
I lifted the sun, the moon, the stars.
I lifted the sky.
I lifted the cosmos with all its dust.
You don't believe me?
Look out your window. It's still there
isn't it, the exquisite world?
Who's to say we didn't lift it,
you and I. Who is to say
that for the smallest instant
it wasn't on our backs, our shoulders?
Just because we didn't know it,
doesn't mean it wasn't there.
Suppose I would have stopped?
Suppose you would have?
Oh, the difference!

About the Author

Richard Nester has twice been a fellow at the Fine Arts Work Center in Provincetown and has made the "tall hike" referred to in the poem "Chestnut Culture" many times. *Red Truck Bear* is his fourth collection of poetry.

www.ingramcontent.com/pod-product-compliance
Lightning Source LLC
Chambersburg PA
CBHW031928080426
42734CB00007B/594